MW01101438

The
PATH *to*
Forgiveness

Daily Reflections, Actions, & Prayers

REV. PAUL BOUDREAU

TWENTY
THIRD 23rd
PUBLICATIONS

Introduction

So far, fifth grade had been the worst year of Sarah's ten-year-old life. She told me that she loved school. The problem was her teacher, Mrs. Nickerson. Sarah didn't know why, but from the very first day of school, it seemed like Mrs. Nickerson had it in for her. Sarah was a good student, but Mrs. Nickerson constantly found fault with her and criticized her openly in the classroom.

Sarah wanted so much to make things right with her teacher. Because she was a thoughtful Catholic, Sarah knew that the first step toward reconciliation with her teacher was forgiveness. But forgiveness was hard. She didn't feel like forgiving Mrs. Nickerson. But she was going to work at it. Lent would be coming after Christmas vacation and Sarah hoped that the season would be a good time to get in shape forgiveness-wise. After all, she thought, that's what being a Catholic is all about.

God is love and love shows itself most beautifully in forgiveness. Forgiveness is what we celebrate during this season of Lent. Forgiveness is always what we celebrate. Our Lord poured out the cup of his blood—"for you and for all," he said—so that our sins would be forgiven. Sarah drank from that cup, and she knew that somehow she would have to share that cup with Mrs. Nickerson.

I wrote this little booklet on the days of Lent for Sarah, for myself, and for you. I hope it will help all of us find new meaning in this holy season. For each day there is a passage from the gospel, a reflection, a little something to do, and a short prayer. By the grace of God, may it be a blessing for us as we take the journey of forgiveness and arrive together at Easter joy.

Twenty-Third Publications, A Division of Bayard, One Montauk Avenue, Suite 200, New London, CT 06320, (860) 437-3012 or (800) 321-0411, www.23rdpublications.com

ISBN 978-1-58595-724-8

The Real You

"When you pray, go to your inner room, close the door, and pray to your Father in secret." MATTHEW 6:6

There's a place deep down inside of us where we truly are the person we are. The person we show on the outside is the person we think others will like, or that others expect us to be. Or that person on the outside is the one that leaks out of us when we're tired or frustrated or upset.

Our inner room is the place sometimes referred to as "the ground of our being," our original selves created in God's own image. It's who we were as little kids before all the layers of doubts, fears, and worldly concerns blotted out the reality of our true selves. But we know it's there. It's the reason why we feel so bad when we behave in ways that are not true. It's what we refer to when we say that people don't really understand us, or that someone doesn't know who we really are. And that's true, because we hide.

But God knows who we are. God is aware of the reality of what is inside of us, our original selves that God created. It's where we meet God in prayer. When Jesus says to go to our inner room and pray, that's what he's talking about.

Prayer is one of the big three disciplines of Lent. It is our commitment to go to our inner room every day to meet with God and to tell God what it's like to live our lives. And to ask God to help us become the people we really want to be. Our original selves.

ACT OF LOVE

Along with the Our Father or the Hail Mary today, tell God what it's like to be who you are. Use your own words. God knows you.

PRAYER OF FAITH

O Lord, you have wonderfully made me. Help me to find again the person you created me to be. Keep me ever in your grace. Amen.

Candy or Beets

"What profit is there for one to gain the whole world yet lose or forfeit oneself?" LUKE 9:25

I used to give up candy for Lent. It seemed like the obvious thing to do because growing up in my family, you had to give up something. And you couldn't just give up something you didn't particularly care for, like beets. You had to give up something you really loved, something that would really challenge you to practice self-discipline.

I maintained this lenten practice well into my adulthood, even after I lost my taste for the sweet stuff. Then something happened to change everything. I had an episode of road rage. I got so mad at another driver on the freeway for cutting me off that I lost control of my temper. I started tailgating the other guy and making some very uncharitable gestures, if you know what I mean.

Well, that got my attention. I realized that I loved to be the king of the road. It didn't matter that I was being a bigger jerk than the other guy. All that mattered was my way. So the following Lent I gave up my spot on the road. For forty days my rightful place on the freeway was up for grabs. After all, why trade in my immortal soul for twenty feet of pavement? It was harder to do than I thought. It took a lot of tries before I started to get it right.

Today I am a much more peaceful driver. Instead of cursing the idiots on the road, I bless them. I mean, they certainly need it.

ACT OF LOVE

There's more to fasting than cutting out things that will help you to lose weight. Give up something you hang onto at the price of your own peace and wellbeing.

PRAYER OF FAITH

Lord, help me to be a docile soul, to take up my cross and surrender my will to yours. May the way of Jesus give me hope. Amen.

A Lenten Proposal

"Can the wedding guests mourn as long as the bridegroom is with them?" MATTHEW 9:15

Carmen came to me all upset. Her boyfriend, Pete, had proposed to her the night before and she was thrilled. Of course she said YES. Pete was the love of her life and she was hoping he would ask soon. Now that he had popped the question, Carmen's mind was filled with all the possibilities that lay ahead. She had shared the good news with her mother, who was very pleased. But she reminded Carmen that it was Lent and she wasn't supposed to be too happy.

But Carmen just couldn't put a lid on her happiness. The season of Lent would probably be spent planning for a fabulous summer wedding. So her problem was, how could she be sad when it was such a time of joy? The answer was that she couldn't. And she needn't be too concerned that her mood didn't seem to match the season.

Lent is a time for happiness too. In the celebration of the lenten Mass, the first preface, the prayer before the Holy, Holy, Holy, expresses the church's thankfulness to God that "each year you give us this joyful season when we prepare to celebrate the paschal mystery with mind and heart renewed." Joy is the other side of the repentance coin. We repent because we are forgiven. We are happy because we have been reconciled with God. Carmen can spend her Lent in joyful hope of the coming of her salvation, and the coming of her wedding!

ACT OF LOVE

Choose something to be glad about today. After all, it's Lent, a joyful season!

PRAYER OF FAITH

Dear God, make me joyful this Lent. Keep me mindful of the great mercy you have shown me and the great love with which you hold me dear. I am sorry for my sins, but grateful for your forgiveness. Amen.

Here Comes the Devil

"I have not come to call the righteous to repentance but sinners." LUKE 5:32

"O Father, the devil is after me. I just know it." Ted came to confession deeply troubled by what seemed to be a constant temptation to think ill of people, to harbor uncharitable thoughts about his family, his friends, his neighbors, and his coworkers. "I must be a wicked person," he lamented, "for the devil to be tempting me like this."

Well, of course the devil was after Ted. Why wouldn't he be? Ted was a fine, upstanding man, a blessing to his family, and a devout member of the church. The reason the devil was after him was not because Ted was an evil person. Heck, if Ted were a bad guy, he'd be right where the devil wanted him and the devil would leave him alone. But because Ted was a good guy, the devil was trying to take him down.

So I had an idea. I told Ted that whenever he was tempted to think ill of someone, he should bless that person. Like "God bless my boss," or "God bless my mother-in-law." It would drive the devil crazy! I saw Ted several weeks later and he said the plan was working great. The devil still tempted him, but he used the opportunity to do something good. "I know I'm a sinner. That's why God is merciful to me," he told me. "But with the devil after me, I know I can be a saint."

ACT OF LOVE

Today, see your evil thoughts as an opportunity for grace. When an uncharitable thought pops into your mind, welcome it with a prayer. The devil will have a fit!

PRAYER OF FAITH

Heavenly Father, you give me the strength to control my thoughts, my actions, and the things I say. Help me today to be a good witness of your grace. Amen.

Bring On the Angels

He was among wild beasts, and the angels ministered to him. MARK 1:13

I had a hard day at church today. Oh, it's possible, you know. Church can be just like your workplace, your school, your neighborhood, or even your family. People are people and sometimes the best of them can get a little weird. It must have been the full moon or something because I felt I was getting more than my share of grief.

One thing I've learned over the years, however, is that when I'm among the wild beasts, the angels minister to me. It's true. And it's true for you, too. Whenever life is starting to pile up, and there are always days when it does, we've got angels taking care of us and giving us what we need to get through the day.

Now I know there are some people who don't believe in angels, least of all not the ones who are sitting on our shoulders and looking out for us. But belief in the things that are unseen is part of our creed, part of our Catholic faith. Plus, if we are united with Jesus Christ in baptism, if the same Spirit in him is in us, if we are made children of God through our communion with Jesus, then we, like the Lord, have angels ministering to us. We may not see them, but they're there, guiding us when things are uncertain, calming us when things heat up, comforting us when everybody else seems to be against us. As it was God's will for Jesus, so it is God's will for us.

ACT OF LOVE

Carry something around with you today—like an angel on your shoulder—to remind yourself of God's abiding love for you and God's care for you.

PRAYER OF FAITH

Dear God, send your holy angels to watch over me today. When I need your help, may your angels take care of me and provide for my needs. Amen.

Taking Care of Jesus

*"Amen, I say to you, whatever you did for one of
these least brothers of mine, you did for me."* MATTHEW 25:40

It was the most difficult thing Blanche ever had to do. When her husband Tom came home from the hospital after his cancer surgery, the prognosis wasn't good. Caring for him at home would be hard. But Blanche made the commitment and she saw it through to the end.

When the priest came to anoint Tom, he told her then that the sacrament was the outward sign of the hidden reality of Christ in Tom's suffering and dying. The title "Christ," after all, means "the anointed one." Just as Christ was anointed to suffer and die for us, so now Tom was anointed to be the visible sign of Christ among us. Tom's suffering and death was the suffering and death of Christ made visible in the sacrament.

Blanche came to realize that in her care for Tom she was caring for Christ. All her hard, frustrating work, all her heartache, all her struggles to keep Tom at home and give him comfort during his final days was in service to her God, and she would not go without her reward. The best part was that just as Tom suffered and died with Christ, so he would rise with him and she would see him again.

After the funeral Blanche was full of sadness, but at the same time she was radiant with joy. What better thing could she have done with her life than serve the one who had suffered and died for her!

ACT OF LOVE

Today you will have opportunities to serve God through caring for God's lowly ones. Care for them as you would care for Christ.

PRAYER OF FAITH

*Father, I thank you that you have shown yourself to me in the poor
and suffering of the world. Help me to always see your presence in
them. Amen.*

Spiritual Wallflowers

"If you forgive their transgressions,
your heavenly Father will forgive you" MATTHEW 6:14

Imagine going to a party at a friend's house and then just sitting in a corner and not saying anything to anybody. Or how about attending a sporting event and reading a book while everybody else is enjoying the game and cheering for their team. Or perhaps you might picture yourself at a movie and snoozing through the whole picture while listening to your favorite tunes on your headset.

In the same way we can become wallflowers at the party of fulfillment that is called forgiveness. What I mean is that we can imagine that we're forgiven, but we don't go out of our way to do any forgiving. In reality, forgiveness is a dynamic; it is the energy of divine mercy in which we participate. If I need to be forgiven—and I most surely do—then I need also to forgive. It's not a one-way street. Forgiveness is like the air we breathe. It does no good simply to breathe it in. To get the full effect and benefit from the life-giving qualities of forgiveness, we must breathe out as much as we breathe in.

Jesus taught about the kingdom of God in terms of a party. In his parables, the invitations go out, but the guests don't show up. In the same way we can be invited to the party of forgiveness, but fail to show up when we don't forgive.

ACT OF LOVE

There are plenty of opportunities to forgive that will come your way today and you need to be alert and ready for them. At the end of the day, tally up the score and see how you did.

PRAYER OF FAITH

Help me, O merciful Lord, to be a forgiving person today. I need your forgiveness as much as others need mine. Amen.

Attracting Flies

"Just as Jonah became a sign to the Ninevites,
so will the Son of Man be to this generation." LUKE 11:30

Like all mothers, my mother had her sayings, little mottos that we kids would hear her repeat at least once a day, if not more. One of her dictums was: "You can attract more flies with honey than with vinegar." As a child, I wondered why anyone would want to attract flies. But later in life her words took on meaning. I discovered that I could attract people and make them my friends by being nice to them.

The "sign of Jonah" that Jesus was talking about in the gospel was more in keeping with the idea of attracting flies with honey. Nineveh, you see, was the hated enemy of Jonah and his people. Jonah's mission was to be the honey that would attract them and transform them from being enemies into being friends. It was a daunting task because Jonah had to walk through their city warning them of the coming judgment of God. No wonder Jonah tried to escape the assignment and ended up in the belly of the whale!

Truth be told, we are sometimes enemies of God. When my thoughts or my words or my actions are contrary to the love of God, or when I fail to think, speak, or act for the sake of God's love, I am God's enemy. To me, then, God reveals the "Sign of the Cross." Jesus is the honey; I am the fly.

ACT OF LOVE

Today, do one nice thing for somebody you're not particularly fond of. A blessing, a word of encouragement, or an act of kindness will make you like the sign of Jonah.

PRAYER OF FAITH

Jesus, my Savior, you willingly gave yourself up to suffering and death for me. May my life today be a sign to others of your infinite love for all people. Amen.

God the Good Grandpa

*"If you who are wicked know how to give good gifts to your children,
how much more will your heavenly Father give
good things to those who ask him!"* MATTHEW 7:11

What a burden of sorrow some grandparents carry for their children and grandchildren. They raise their kids to be faithful Catholics. Then, somewhere along the way, the kids lose their faith and stop going to church. Even when the kids get married and start having kids of their own, they don't include religion in family life. The grandchildren don't get baptized and grandparents are at a loss as to what to do.

The problem is not that we've been bad parents. God knows we've all done our very best. We know how to be good parents. But can we be better parents to our kids than God is to them? There's the catch. We're pretty confident in our own parenting skills, but we don't seem to trust God's.

The fact of the matter is that God is a far better parent than we can ever hope to be. And God has the situation well in hand. God promised to watch over our kids and lead them to salvation. We're called to put our trust in God's faithfulness to fulfill this promise, not necessarily in our kids' ability to fulfill our expectations. That's why we have a heavenly Father and a Blessed Mother, so that when our human weakness kicks in, we have the divine presence to bail us out.

ACT OF LOVE

Put your holy cards together with the photos of your kids as a reminder that God is leading them to salvation in a way you haven't been able to figure out yet.

PRAYER OF FAITH

O God, I thank you for the gift of my family. Help me to trust in your care for them. Help me to believe in your divine parenting skills. Amen.

11

PARENTING

Can We Do It?

"Unless your righteousness surpasses that of the scribes and Pharisees, you will not enter the Kingdom of heaven." MATTHEW 5:20

"I don't know what it is, Father," the fellow in the bow tie said to me, "I just keep committing the same sins over and over again. I 'firmly resolve' to 'amend my life' each time I come to confession, but it's just no use. I'm back again a week later confessing the same sins." The man's eyes filled up with tears and his face contorted in a futile attempt to contain his emotions, but he broke down and wept. "I'm just so afraid, " he cried, "that I won't make it to heaven if I keep up like this."

I don't blame the guy for feeling wretched about his sins. If getting into heaven depended on my righteousness, I wouldn't have a snowflake's chance in…well, you know what I mean. But thank God getting into heaven is not a function of my righteousness, but rather of the mercy of God and the sacrifice of Jesus Christ. As the gospel says, if entering the kingdom was a matter of righteousness, our righteousness would have to exceed that of the scribes and Pharisees, the most righteous guys on earth!

My friend in the bowtie would like to make it on his own merits. But I told him he needs to realize that we're granted entry into heaven by the grace of God, not by any righteousness of our own. Our sins are overcome by God's forgiveness, not by our efforts not to sin. We need to practice virtue and avoid sin, but our hope is always in the Lord.

ACT OF LOVE

Spend today in gratitude. Once every hour, thank God for forgiving all your sins. Then make a good confession this weekend if you can.

PRAYER OF FAITH

Thank you for your many gifts to me, O Lord. Most of all, I thank you for the forgiveness of my sins. Help me to be virtuous, and to live in gratitude all the days of my life. Amen.

Latella the Hun

"Love your enemies, and pray for those who persecute you,
that you may be children of your heavenly Father." MATTHEW 5:44–45

Bernice hates to go to work. Her boss, Latella, constantly hassles her about everything under the sun. She criticizes Bernice's work and even makes comments about the clothes Bernice wears and the color of her hair!

Bernice would love to quit, but she needs the job. It provides medical insurance for her husband and kids. But spending eight hours a day with Latella the Hun is a real burden. She prays every day that something will happen to take her boss out of the picture.

Bernice has an opportunity to take a big step toward becoming a better Christian woman. She needs to recognize that the cross she bears is a communion with the cross of Jesus Christ. God loves Latella and wants what is best for her. Bernice needs to know that, and her prayer should reflect that reality. After all, who better to pray for Latella's wellbeing than the one who is suffering from her persecution? It sounds a little counter-intuitive, but that is the paradox of the cross. When we suffer for the sake of others as Jesus suffered for us, we grow in holiness.

ACT OF LOVE

There are people in your life that you need to pray for, people that you don't necessarily like, people that give you a hard time, but God loves these people. Write down three names now and ask God's blessings for them.

PRAYER OF FAITH

Dear Lord, I'm making this prayer today for you-know-who. Even though I don't like this person very much—and you know why I don't—I'm going to ask you to bless this person. Amen.

Hey Down There

Then a cloud came, casting a shadow over them; from the cloud came a voice,
"This is my beloved Son. Listen to him." MARK 9:7

For a long time I thought the clouds that came into my life blocked out the light of God's presence. I felt that the shadows of sadness and depression caused by my day-to-day difficulties, and my own repeated failures to live life in a morally responsible and virtuous way, were keeping me from enjoying the blessings of God. Nothing could have been further from the truth.

I discovered in the Bible that when the clouds come and the shadows fall, it is God who is speaking to me. Every time the cloud shows up in the Bible, like in Exodus 40:34–35 when the cloud filled the meeting tent, or 1 Kings 8:10 when the cloud came to rest on the newly built temple, or in today's gospel story of the Transfiguration, God is present and in communion with us.

The presence of God is always a mystery. Hence the cloud. But Jesus reveals God as a paradox: the blind see, the lame walk, the deaf hear, the virgin conceives, sinners are forgiven, the dead rise. So when I think God is not present, God most certainly is very present. When my life feels like it's in the deepest darkness, God's light is shining brightly. When difficulty and sadness come my way, God is nearest to me, helping me and showing me the way.

ACT OF LOVE

Count your troubles today. God doesn't will these difficulties to come, but they do. And when they come, God is there to bless you.

PRAYER OF FAITH

Dear God, I'm not sure I want to actually thank you for the trouble in my life. But I do want to thank you for all the help you give me. Amen.

GOD'S PRESENCE - CLOUDS

Get Rich Quick

*"The measure with which you measure will in return
be measured out to you."* LUKE 6:38

God is a God of balance who makes everything work together to bring about a certain balance we call "peace." For instance, in the story of creation in Genesis, God creates light and darkness, day and night, sky and earth, sea and dry land, male and female. Get the picture? For everything that is, there is something else that pairs with it, an opposite that balances. There is up and down, left and right, on and off, in and out, good and bad, and so on.

This peace of God has its expression in the way we live. It is also, as Jesus teaches, a paradox: "The last shall be first and the first shall be last." In today's gospel Jesus tells us to "give and it will be given to you," just as he says in another place, "seek and you shall find." Plus the measure of our giving will be the same as the measure of our receiving. If, therefore, we give sparingly, we will receive sparingly. But if we give abundantly, then we will receive abundantly. How about that?

This realization has certainly changed the way I give. I used to give based on how much I could afford. I still do, but now it's the other way around. What I can afford is based on what I need. If I need more, then I give more. It's scary sometimes. But if it were easy, everybody would be doing it.

ACT OF LOVE

By giving, you determine how much God gives to you. Need more time? Give more time today. Need more help? Give more help today. It all adds up.

PRAYER OF FAITH

Almighty God, you gave everything for me. Help me to give back to you in the measure with which I wish to receive. Amen.

GIVING

Here, Have a Burden

"They tie up heavy burdens hard to carry and lay them on people's shoulders, but they will not lift a finger to move them." MATTHEW 23:4

Jesus warns his disciples to beware of the guys who like to dress up in religious garb and wear marks of respect, enjoy titles of reverence and places of honor in the assembly. Wait a minute: We're supposed to look out for those guys? But we put them in charge!

It's no secret that the greatest scandals in our church have come at the hands of our leadership. If someone on the edge of church life, someone who doesn't participate all that much, does something wrong, it's no big deal. Nobody even notices. But if a priest or a bishop gets off track, then it's a major event, a public disgrace. And well it should be. If I'm going to accept such a position of authority and responsibility, I'd better make sure I have all my moral ducks in a row and am committed to the way of excellence.

Did you ever notice that the big issues in our religion seem to be about sex, marriage, and having babies? And that the leaders of our church don't do sex, get married, or have babies? I wonder if this is what Jesus meant when he said that they load burdens on others that they don't carry themselves. Just a thought. But if the Lord's words are to have any impact in our lives, they must be seen for what they are. The leaders of our church, myself included, need to take some lessons in humility.

ACT OF LOVE

If you're not a clergy person, maybe you're a parent, or a manager, or a teacher. Today it's time for a reality check. God put you there to serve. See how often you can serve today.

PRAYER OF FAITH

O Lord, keep me humble. I really want to serve you by serving others. Help me use the gifts of respect and honor and responsibility you give me today for the good of all. Amen.

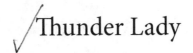Thunder Lady

"Whoever wishes to be great among you shall be your servant."
MATTHEW 20:26

I love the story of Mrs. Zebedee. She is the unnamed mother of the apostles James and John, the wife of their father, Zebedee. She seems to have had quite a reputation in the early church. In the gospel of Mark, Jesus nicknames James and John *Boanerges*, which means "sons of thunder." Do you suppose he was referring to their mother?

Anyway, today Mrs. Zebedee is on the warpath, rousting Jesus with a request that he give the top spots in the coming kingdom to her sons. Of course her understanding is that Jesus will usher in an earthly kingdom, like Camelot or something. In such a kingdom, the top positions would be like vice king or prime minister, offices of great authority. In other words, Mrs. Zebedee, like any mother, wants what is best for her sons.

And so does Jesus want what is best for his friends. But what is best in the world isn't necessarily what is best in the kingdom—for the world is passing away, but the kingdom is coming. And the gospel paradox is always at work. What is gained in the world is lost in the kingdom, and vice versa. So what is best for Mrs. Zebedee's sons are positions of service. The word in the language of the gospels is "slave," the lowest position in the social order. That's the best place to be.

ACT OF LOVE

Take an honest measure of your hopes for yourself. Then imagine how to do it, not in terms of the world, but in terms of the coming kingdom.

PRAYER OF FAITH

Keep me humble, heavenly Father. May the greatness you give me today be used in the service of all. Amen.

Pay Attention

*"Lying at his door was a poor man named Lazarus...
who would gladly have eaten his fill of the scraps that fell
from the rich man's table."* LUKE 16:20–21

"Father, how come...?" Most questions to me about God, church, or whatever, seem to start off this way. But this particular question kind of hit home. "Father," my questioner went on, "how come God lets so many of the little children starve in Africa?"

Fair enough question. But the premise is all wrong. God doesn't let the children in Africa starve. God has a system set up to take care of all the needs of the world. He has organized his people into a network of caregivers and then given them a directive: Feed the hungry. So there you go. God doesn't let the kids in Africa starve. God says, "Feed them." The real question is: How are we doing?

God gives us everything we need. We certainly have enough to share and the means through which to share it. We spend billions trying to kill people; it would seem we have the resources to save a few. We've got way more than enough food, unless we eat twice as much as we need, which is often the case. So when we see tragedy, like the disaster in Darfur, unfold, we know that God is trying to stop it. We just have to realize who it is that God is calling to do the work.

ACT OF LOVE

Stand on the scale and take a look in the mirror. Have you been eating more than your share? Fasting is a discipline of Lent. Cut back on your portions today.

PRAYER OF FAITH

Loving God, you give us so much, and you call us to serve you as good stewards of your many gifts to us. Help us to see in the abundance on our tables the call to feed the hungry of the world. Amen.

Fish Lips

"When vintage time drew near, he sent his servants to the tenants to obtain his produce." MATTHEW 21:34

"God made me to know Him, to love Him, and to serve Him in this world, and to be happy with Him forever in the next." Recognize that? It's the answer to Question #6 of the Baltimore Catechism, "Why did God make you?" Most of us growing up Catholic in the 40s, 50s, and 60s, learned our religion from that little book. The answer kind of sticks in our memory because the good sisters put it in there with such energy. I remember Sr. Faleeta squeezing my mouth into fish lips because I didn't get the answer right. Well I'm here to tell you, I've been getting that answer right ever since.

Which is important because we are indeed put into this world to know, love, and serve the God who created us. We are to bring God's graces to bear in the world, right where it needs it. So God gives us a rich supply of food. God gives us liberty and democracy. God gives us prosperity. And when the Lord comes again in glory, he'll be looking for the fruit this abundance has produced.

So what happens if we use all the food to increase our body size? What if we fail to create a just society? What if we use the money to remodel the bathroom or take a fabulous vacation? Well, I don't know. What would you do if you were God?

ACT OF LOVE

God gives you an abundance of time, money, and ability that you are to use in the service of God. Today, put a little time, a little effort, and a little money into fulfilling your purpose.

PRAYER OF FAITH

O God my Creator, you have wonderfully made me and given me many things. Help me to fulfill my mission so that I can be happy with you in the world to come. Amen.

Forgiveness Comes First

*"While he was still a long way off, his father caught sight of him,
and was filled with compassion."* LUKE 15:20

Jeremy wasn't going to give in and neither was his cousin Jeff. Oh, they had
gotten into it over one thing or another years ago, something to do with the
keys to their grandfather's car. They were both probably at fault, but Jeremy
wasn't going to forgive Jeff unless Jeff came forward. And Jeff wasn't going to
let Jeremy off the hook until Jeremy gave in. Trouble was, they were as close
as brothers and their disagreement was a fly in the ointment of a beautiful
relationship.

Technically they were both right to insist that the other come up with
contrition and confession. At the same time they needed to consider uni-
lateral forgiveness for the sake of their relationship. There are plenty of in-
stances in the gospels of Jesus forgiving people who never say a word. There's
the story about the woman caught in adultery (John 8:3–11,) the paralytic
(Matthew 9:2,) and of course the Lord's famous prayer of forgiveness for
those who were crucifying him (Luke 23:34.)

It's always a good idea to be ready to forgive others without any prompt-
ing from those who have injured you. Why? Because it not only lifts the
weight from the other person's shoulders, it also relieves your own burden.
At any rate, sin is better off forgiven than held bound. It's the difference between an open wound and one that is healed.

ACT OF LOVE

There's probably someone you know who needs your forgiveness.
Today is the day to forgive. Why carry the hurt for another moment?

PRAYER OF FAITH

*Father, your Son poured out the cup of his Blood for the forgiveness of
our sins. Help me to forgive those who trespass against me, as you have
forgiven my trespasses. Amen.*

Mulberry Tree Faith

"Destroy this temple and in three days I will raise it up." JOHN 2:19

I'm always amazed at the vitality of the mulberry tree. It's a common landscape tree where I live in the southwest because it is so robust and can survive desert heat and drought. Each winter it can be cut way back. Some people cut off all the branches so that there are just a few sticks left protruding from the trunk. To look at one you'd think it was dead. Yet each spring it sprouts new shoots and by mid summer a whole new tree is formed. I know one guy who cut his fruitless mulberry down, right flush with the ground. But the next spring it sprouted from the stump and started growing a new tree.

Life is like that. Rooted in the eternal existence of God, life keeps coming back. The cycles of death and resurrection continue year after year, reminding us that God is the beginning and the end of all things, and we need not be afraid. It is necessary for things to be torn down and built up in order to continue. Just as the mulberry tree renews itself each year, so must our lives and the lives of our loved ones be from time to time torn down so that they can be built up again.

Whenever I see young people stop going to church, I know that the faith of their youth is being torn down so that God can build up a strong, mature faith in them. Don't be afraid. Life is eternal. What is torn down on one day can be raised up in three.

ACT OF LOVE

On the way home today, stop by the supermarket and pick up some flowers. Let those flowers remind you of the new ones that grew up when those were cut down.

PRAYER OF FAITH

You create all things, O Lord, so that your eternal life may be expressed in our world. When I see something pass away, help me to know that you are raising up something new and wonderful. Amen.

Blessing the Bad Guy

"There were many lepers in Israel during the time of Elisha the prophet; yet not one of them was cleansed, but only Naaman the Syrian."

LUKE 4:27

It wasn't all that long ago when we were taught that everybody who wasn't Catholic was going to hell. I remember as a kid coming home one day and saying to my mother, "They taught us today in catechism that the Protestants won't go to heaven. Is that true?" I found it was always a good idea to check with my mother about things that I heard. She was wise and devout and always seemed to have the right answer.

"It's what the church teaches," she said. "But I don't believe it." Now this was from a woman who went to Mass every day and prayed the rosary. Turns out she was right, as usual. No matter how hard we sometimes try, we can never get around our Lord's command to love our enemies.

Jesus pointed out to his hometown congregation that God cared for the hated enemies of Israel, healing them and providing for them in their need (See 2 Kings 5:1–17). They were so enraged that they tried to kill Jesus, but he escaped. I wonder what would happen today if the priest announced at Mass that God loved the enemies of America and cared for them. Probably the same thing. The love of our enemies and the acceptance of those who oppose us is still something we Catholics have to come to terms with.

ACT OF LOVE

So who do you exclude from the love of God? Spend some time today repenting of your judgmental attitude and getting back on track.

PRAYER OF FAITH

O Lord, my heart is sometimes hard toward those I count as my enemies. Please transform me by the power of your grace so that I may love as you love. Amen.

The Zillion Dollar Debt

"Should you not have had pity on your fellow servant, as I had pity on you?"
MATTHEW 18:33

Eddie and Ryan were brothers. But they weren't speaking to each other. I'm not too sure what the problem was; they both had different stories. But by all accounts it wasn't much. But they got it into their heads that one wasn't going to forgive the other without an apology. Since they both lived in the same town, and went to the same church (mine), it was presenting a problem for their family and their parish.

Today's gospel says that the servant owed his master "a huge amount." A literal translation of the ancient language would be "10,000 talents." A talent of gold in Judea at that time would weigh in at around 200 pounds. Ten thousand talents would make that a thousand TONS…of gold! So, you do the math and that's a lot of scratch. The "much smaller amount" the other servant owed can be translated literally as "100 denarion," roughly a hundred days wages. That's no small debt for anyone, but doable. In any event, what the second servant owed was paltry compared to what the first servant owed.

The numbers demand that we forgive each other. All the time. For everything. There is no offense done to us that can at all compare with the offense we do to God. So Eddie and Ryan need to get on the stick and forgive each other before it's too late.

ACT OF LOVE

Guess what: it's forgiveness time again. Somebody is going to cut you off on the freeway or the person ahead of you in the supermarket "15-item" express lane is going to have 23 items. Get to work and start forgiving.

PRAYER OF FAITH

Dear God, you forgive my huge debt. You put aside my sins so that I may live in your peace. When others offend me, remind me of my mission of witness. May I forgive as I have been forgiven. Amen.

First Things First

"Whoever obeys and teaches these commandments will be called greatest in the Kingdom of heaven." MATTHEW 5:19

Living a righteous life is not optional for the People of God. Even though we have been set free from the law and live in the forgiveness of our sins, we still need to conduct our lives virtuously and do good. It is by acting with justice, by treating others with compassion, by respecting the dignity of human life in all its forms, by thinking good thoughts, saying good words, and doing good things that we best serve God and witness to the presence of God's Holy Spirit within us.

At the same time, we are called to live beyond the law, recognizing that in Christ there is something greater than the law, and that the law was made for the sake of humanity, not humanity for the sake of the law. (See Mark 2:23–28.) In the story of the woman caught in adultery, the law demanded that she be put to death. But Jesus got her off the hook. (See John 8:3–11.) And remember, it was according to the law that they crucified Jesus. (See John 19:7.)

So there will be times in our lives when the law will demand one thing while mercy and compassion will demand something else. If our lives are to be a witness to God's justice, then we must be merciful and compassionate. If we inflict the law on others, the law will be inflicted on us. If we judge others according to the law, we will be judged according to the law. And none of us can survive that.

ACT OF LOVE

Today there will be more people we need to forgive at work, on the freeway, and in our families. The mercy shown to us, we must show to others.

PRAYER OF FAITH

Lord, you have forgiven me so much. Help me today to be merciful as you are merciful. Amen.

Off the Hook

Joseph, her husband, since he was a righteous man, yet unwilling to expose her to shame, decided to divorce her quietly. MATTHEW 1:19

Today is the feast of Saint Joseph, the husband of the Blessed Virgin Mary. The Bible says that he was a righteous man, which means he kept the commandments. He knew, by the fact that Mary was pregnant and the baby was not his, that Mary was seemingly in gross violation of the sixth commandment, "Thou shalt not commit adultery." And the consequences were grave. According to the law, a woman who had committed adultery should be put to death. (See Deuteronomy 22:20–21.)

But Joseph was also a just man, so he decided that while he must divorce Mary to preserve the sanctity of his family, he would do so on the QT in order to shield Mary from the law and protect her from a public trial that would most certainly result in her being executed.

But God revealed to Joseph that in order to fulfill his devotion to all that is holy and good, Joseph would be required to go even further. He would keep Mary as his wife and bring up the baby as his own. This was an extraordinary step for even a righteous man. He would have to step out beyond the context of his own religion in order to do the will of God. That he did so makes him one of the greatest saints of all time.

ACT OF LOVE

If you get a chance, stop by a church today and find the statue of St. Joseph. He's usually the guy with the lily. Tell him what you think of his righteous act and ask him to help you follow his example in your life.

PRAYER OF FAITH

Dear Lord, through the intercession of St. Joseph, help me to be a righteous person. May I do your will today, even if it means going beyond what I think is right. Amen.

Missing the Kingdom

When Jesus saw that (the man) answered with understanding, he said to him,
"You are not far from the kingdom of God." MARK 12:34

I missed my bus the other day. I figured I had plenty of time, but just as I was walking around the corner, there was my bus at the stop taking on the last passenger in line. I ran as fast as I could, but before I could get there, the bus pulled away. I was not far from making it; I only missed it by a few feet. But I might as well have missed it by a mile.

So when the Lord told the fellow, who agreed with him about loving God and neighbor being the greatest commandment, that he was "not far" from the kingdom of God, that just about blew my mind. Not far? Are you kidding? You mean I can love God with everything I've got and love my neighbor as myself and end up "not far" from the kingdom? Thanks a lot. I might as well end up a mile away.

It just goes to show you that the kingdom of God is not about conforming to the commandments. It's about conforming to Christ. Sure, he loved God and his neighbor, but he loved more than that. He loved you and me with his life. He gave up everything for us. That goes way beyond the commandment. That's the kind of love that will put us on the bus.

ACT OF LOVE

Consider your love for God. Do you love God with your whole heart, soul, mind, and strength? Probably not. Neither do I, truth be told. I spend a lot of myself loving other things. Now consider God's love for you. Can you live in that love today?

PRAYER OF FAITH

Heavenly Father, you love me with an infinite love and your Son Jesus gave his life for me. Help me today to bask in the extraordinary light of your love. Amen.

Me? Sin?

Jesus addressed this parable to those who were convinced of their own righteousness. LUKE 18:9

People like to come to me for confession because I don't ask them too many questions. I usually just give them a three-and-three, absolve them, and send them out the door. I figure they know the difference between right and wrong. All I can say is, "Stop committing those sins." Besides, I've got Mass coming up and twenty more people waiting in line. With all devout and reverent expediency, I've got to move things along.

So it's kind of annoying when somebody comes in and starts confessing his or her own righteousness. It goes something like this: "Well, Father, I try to be good. I go to Mass every Sunday. I don't swear. I don't steal anything. I don't cheat on my spouse," etc. My all-time favorite is: "I'm 86 years-old, Father, so I don't sin no more." Huh?

Look, we're all sinners. It says so right in the Bible: "All have sinned and are deprived of the glory of God." (See Romans 3:23.) It would just be a joke to stand before God and declare my righteousness. God would laugh at me. If I truly believe in "one baptism for the forgiveness of sin" as I say every Sunday, then I don't mind confessing my sins. I don't have to try to look good in the eyes of God; certainly not the eyes of the priest to whom I am confessing. So how about we just confess our sins, do penance, and amend our lives. Amen.

ACT OF LOVE

When you go to confession, confess your sins and not your righteousness. Don't downplay anything. Put it all out there and be absolved of everything.

PRAYER OF FAITH

Father, in Christ you forgive all my sins. That just lifts up my heart. Thank you for your mercy. Help me to make a good confession this Lent. Amen.

Forgiveness Awaits

God did not send his Son into the world to condemn the world,
but that the world might be saved through him. JOHN 3:17

Todd was in a fix. He loved his wife, Rebecca, but he had done a really stupid thing. He was having an affair. He tried to tell himself that it just sort of happened. But it didn't just sort of happen. Every step along the way he had surrendered to his own ego and his own carnal desires. It began with thoughts and evolved into words and actions. He calculated, he initiated, he invited, and he accepted invitations. Soon he was in it so deep that he didn't know how to get out of it. And he hated himself for it.

Now his life had become a web of lies and deceptions. He stayed out late nights, pretending to be at work. He missed his kids' sporting events and recitals. He even started taking weekend "business trips." His relationship with his wife and family, and even his friends, was spiraling downward. He was depressed. His double life was killing him.

I hope this story doesn't sound too familiar to you. Unfortunately it's told to me by many men and women, good people who have made bad choices. All I can tell them is that God doesn't condemn them; God wants to save them. And that forgiveness awaits their repentance. It is with this knowledge of God's love for them that they can break out of their prison of sin and begin a new life in the freedom of God's children.

ACT OF LOVE

Joy awaits the sinner who repents. When we bring our wickedness out of the darkness and into the light by confessing our sins, we receive the grace of forgiveness and healing, something we all need. Today God is ready to give new life to you and me.

PRAYER OF FAITH

O God, help me to know the truth about myself that will set me free. Help me to confess my sins and start a new life of grace and holiness. Amen.

Is Doubt Okay?

"Unless you people see signs and wonders, you will not believe." JOHN 4:48

"I just don't feel God's presence in my life anymore," Tara said. She was look-ing for an emotional experience of God. She wanted to believe, but felt that without something real to hold onto, she couldn't bring herself to the faith that she thought she should have. She tried prayer, but the experience was dry and meaningless to her. She joined a prayer group, but was discour-aged when others reported their exuberant consolations while her heart felt empty. She was without the sureness of God's presence and she felt her faith flagging. Why did others experience God in their lives while her own soul languished? She was doubting and was afraid that doubt was a great sin.

Many of us encounter Tara's difficulty with faith and doubt. It's impor-tant to remember that faith and doubt are two sides of the same coin. You can't really believe in God unless there is the possibility of not believing. You can't really say yes to the presence of the Lord unless you have the freedom to say no.

Recall the experience of Mother Teresa. In her letters published last year, she admitted to doubt every day. She, like Tara, didn't feel the presence of God in her ministry among the poor. She had to believe God was there de-spite all evidence to the contrary. Faith is a belief in what we don't see and what we don't feel.

ACT OF LOVE

Look in the mirror. Do you see the presence of Christ? Yet the mys-tery of the Eucharist we share says that he's really there, looking back at you. Can you believe it?

PRAYER OF FAITH

Lord, I do believe. Help me in my unbelief. Though I don't see you or feel you, help me always to believe in you. Amen.

Give It a Rest

"It is the Sabbath, and it is not lawful for you to carry your mat." JOHN 5:10

I heard a story once about a guy who lived across the street from the parish priest. Every Sunday afternoon he would wash his car in his driveway. And every Sunday afternoon the parish priest would walk across the street to hassle him because he was doing work on Sunday.

In the gospel stories, the legal eagles are always getting on somebody's case, especially the Lord's, for doing work on the sabbath. And certainly the story I just told reminds us that there are modern-day law enforcers, even if the priest in the story seemed a little picky.

But there are reasons why God's law calls us to rest. Think for a moment: Do you know somebody who works seven days a week? How would you evaluate that person's life? Is it healthy? Does that person have a quality family life? The Sabbath is God's way of telling us to take it easy. You need your rest. You need a day to relax with your family. All work and no play make for a lousy week. Yeah, the guy carrying his mat in the gospel had a good excuse. And some people need to work seven days straight once in a while. Okay, and your car really does need a wash. But keep in mind the Lord has your best interests in mind. So give it a rest.

ACT OF LOVE

When's the last time you took a day off? I mean a real day off. Get out your calendar and mark a day to just relax and spend some time with the people you love, or just sitting out in the back yard with a good book, enjoying the day. It's God's will for you.

PRAYER OF FAITH

My life can get pretty busy, Lord. And I sometimes forget to give my body, my mind, and my soul a rest. Your love calls me to relax in your love. Thy will be done. Amen.

Mary First, Then You

*"Behold, you will conceive in your womb and bear a son,
and you shall name him Jesus."* LUKE 1:31

Today we celebrate the moment that life on earth began for Jesus in the womb of his mother, the Blessed Virgin Mary. No longer would God simply create humanity and remain separated by the infinite gulf between heaven and earth. From this moment on divinity would take a full share in the enterprise of humanity. The Word of God would become one of us. Eternity would condense into the dimensions of time and space and God would be joined with us in a communion of spirit, flesh, and blood.

Whew! Sounds pretty radical. But God's love is pretty radical. God so loves you and me that God wanted to share our lives completely, and at the same time give us a share in his divinity. So complete is God's love for us that God wanted to experience the one thing we have that God doesn't: death. In other words, God would rather suffer and die than be apart from us.

God's favor for Mary was expressed in her Immaculate Conception, that she herself was conceived without sin at the beginning of her own life. We are favored by God in our baptism, when we were washed clean of sin. Divinity entered Mary's body the same way it enters ours in the mystery of the Eucharist when we eat and drink the Body and Blood of Christ. What a miracle! And it's going on in us right now.

ACT OF LOVE

The next time you go to communion, hear the voice of the angel announcing to you that you bear the Real Presence of Christ within you. How blessed are you!

PRAYER OF FAITH

Father in heaven, I thank you that you have chosen me to be the bearer of Christ in the world. May I let this be done in me according to your word. Amen.

When God Messes Up

*"The works that the Father gave me to accomplish, these works that
I perform testify on my behalf that the Father has sent me."* John 5:36

"I'm a little mad at God right now," Joan confessed, "because my husband
has just been diagnosed with cancer." She had been good, been faithful to
her husband, and had raised her children well. Furthermore, she had never
in her life missed Mass except for illness and had said her rosary every day.
But now it seemed that God was not holding up his end of the bargain.

Joan's anger at God was understandable. Anger at God indicates a lively
relationship with the Lord, open and honest. Truth be told, we all get a little
angry with God once in a while. And God can handle it. God knows all
about anger.

In time Joan would come to understand that her husband's illness wasn't
God's will. Long life and fulfillment are God's will for all people. But as we
read in the Bible, imperfect humanity often thwarts God's will. If people
don't fulfill God's will, how can we expect our imperfect human bodies to
fulfill God's will? This time around, God would accomplish a healing for
Joan's husband. But sooner or later, our imperfections catch up with us and
we suffer and die. It is enough for us, and will be for Joan and her husband,
that, in Christ, God suffers and dies with us.

ACT OF LOVE

Is there something going wrong in your life right now? There usually
is. Understand that God is there for you, struggling with you. Even
in suffering and death, God is present. Rage against the darkness and
God will rage with you.

PRAYER OF FAITH

*God of heaven and earth, you make all things work for our good. Help
me to believe that you will make good come from the trouble in my life.
Amen.*

Where's He From?

"You know me and also know where I am from.
Yet I did not come on my own, but the one who sent me,
whom you do not know, is true." JOHN 7:28

When Rolando Perez and his family moved into town, there was a bit of a buzz. It was an all-white, all-Anglo neighborhood and Rolando's was the first family of a "different" race and a "different" nationality. Most folks in the hood took it in stride. But Carl was angry. He said he didn't like "Mexicans," although Rolando and his family were from El Salvador.

In talk over the fence, Carl started telling neighbors that Rolando's family meant trouble, that "most" crime in the city was committed by "illegals," and that people like Rolando would crowd "our" kids out of the schools.

What Carl didn't realize is that God had sent Rolando and his family into their neighborhood to help Carl and some others step up to the love of God for all people. Carl had been brought up Catholic, but in a family that was prejudiced. He had never unlearned the racism and bigotry he grew up with.

People who suffer oppression because of hatred and fear wear the face of Christ for us. Rolando was "one of these least brothers" with whom the Lord identifies in Matthew 25:40. We think we know where they are from, but we don't. But we do know that Christ is among us in the persons of the lowly.

ACT OF LOVE

At work, in the neighborhood, at school, or in church, we encounter the Lord's lowly sisters and brothers. Make one small change of heart today for Christ's sake.

PRAYER OF FAITH

Dear Lord, I can't help my feelings about others, but I can control my thoughts, my words, and my actions. Help me today to serve you in your lowly ones. Amen.

The Us-Them Thing

"The Christ will not come from Galilee, will he?" JOHN 7:41

It doesn't take a degree in sociology to figure out that in the gospel stories the people of Judea didn't much care for the people of Galilee. It was a north-south thing stemming from a civil war that happened a thousand years before. The southern people of Judea, the Jews, held great animosity toward the people of the north, the Galileans. Isaiah refers to the Galileans as "heathens" (See Isaiah 8:23.) In John 8:48, they call Jesus a "Samaritan," kind of a collective insult for anybody north of the border. Even Galileans themselves didn't like each other. In John 1:46, Nathanael asks if anything good can come out of Nazareth. And he was from Cana, the next town over from Nazareth! The inscription on the Lord's cross, "Jesus the Nazorean, the King of the Jews," was meant to be a mockery.

The town where I grew up maintained a heated rivalry with the folks from the next town. Even people from neighboring parishes were in contention. Our pastor told us once that if we went to Mass at the church across town it would be a mortal sin.

But in the kingdom of God, there is no north or south, east or west. Everybody lives in harmony with each other. All differences are dissolved. In Christ we are all made one in the unity of the Holy Spirit. So we need to get started right now preparing for the coming of the kingdom.

ACT OF LOVE

It's almost impossible to not have some prejudice in us, because that's the way we were brought up. Write down yours on a piece of paper. Then tear it up and throw it away.

PRAYER OF FAITH

You create people of every race, language, and nationality, Lord. And you put us all together to live together in peace. Help me to become an instrument of your peace. Amen.

One or the Other

"Whoever loves his life loses it, and whoever hates his life in this world will preserve it for eternal life." JOHN 12:25

Life in this world is not eternal. On the contrary, earthly life has a beginning and an end from which there is no escape. "So what's the point?" the author of the Old Testament book of Ecclesiastes might ask. And given the perspective of simply the passing world, there is no point: you're born, you live, and you die. "All is vanity" (Ecclesiastes 12:8).

Jesus proclaimed the kingdom of God, a kind of coexisting universe that was not passing away. But it was definitely not the world and you couldn't have both. "You cannot serve two masters," Jesus taught in Luke 16:13. "You cannot serve God and wealth." Plus, in the kingdom, the last of this world are going to be first and the first are going to be last. In the kingdom, the blind of the world see, the lame walk, and the deaf hear; the dead rise, and the virgin is a mother!

So, living to gain the world really is pointless. In fact, it is ultimately a total loss, because while you might gain the whole world, you would lose your own self in the process (Luke 9:25). In the end, when your world passes away, you are left with only yourself, whom you've already traded in for the world; so you end up with nothing.

ACT OF LOVE

Short of everything, what more can you give up for the sake of the coming kingdom? Pick just one thing and let it go. Some day you'll be glad you did.

PRAYER OF FAITH

Lord, teach me to love the things of heaven. May I always live in this passing world with my heart set on the world that will never end. Amen.

Who Is Without Sin?

*"Let the one among you who is without sin be the
first to throw a stone at her."* JOHN 8:7

Theresa came to me in anguish. Her teenaged daughter had just come home from school and announced that she was pregnant. This was Theresa's worst nightmare. She ranted and raved at her daughter and then stormed out of the house. After driving around for a while, she showed up at my door.

Pulling tissues from the box I keep close by where Theresa sat, she dabbed at the streaks of mascara running down her cheeks and poured out her heart. She told me how, years ago when she was still in school, her father had said that if any daughter of his got pregnant, she might as well not come home because she wouldn't be welcome. When Theresa herself got pregnant in her senior year, she took his advice and didn't come home. She went straight to the abortion clinic and ended the pregnancy. Now she was swimming in an ocean of conflicting emotions. She loved her daughter but hated the pregnancy. Her father's voice was still speaking condemnation and rejection in her.

Death was the punishment for the woman's sin in the gospel. But Jesus had mercy on her and let her go free. It would be the same for Theresa and her daughter. When the spirit of judgment arises in our hearts, the spirit of compassion arises also. Theresa had to choose, and in the end, she would choose the part that saved the baby's life.

ACT OF LOVE

Carry a reminder in your pocket today that when you are tempted to judge and condemn another, no matter how great the offense, that the spirit of the Lord is within you, showering the world with compassion.

PRAYER OF FAITH

Lord Jesus, you paid the price for my sins and you teach me to forgive others as I am forgiven. May the forgiveness in me flow out to the world around me. Amen.

Pulpit Pounders

"When you lift up the Son of Man, you will realize that I AM."
JOHN 8:28

I was out of town not too long ago and attended a local church for Sunday Mass. I like to sit in the congregation and get a perspective of what Mass is like from the pewster's point of view. Because I am a priest, just about every Mass I go to has the same guy presiding. So it's important for me to get the occasional different look.

I was almost sorry I did. In his homily, the priest ranted and raved about sinners. He went on and on about all the evil things people do. It was like a throwback to the hellfire and brimstone days. Sure, we need to condemn sin. The church needs to be a moral compass. But a compass is supposed to point where we're going. That being the case, there is a greater need for Catholic preachers to proclaim the good news.

God, the great "I AM," simply is. (See Exodus 3:14.) In God, there is no right or wrong, good or bad. There is only God. From the very beginning, the knowledge of good and evil is not what God intended for creation. It caused conflict, shame, and alienation. (Look up the story surrounding Genesis 3:6–7.) The people flocked to Jesus and they believed in him because he did not distinguish the good from the bad, sinners from saints, but rather demonstrated God's love for all people, good or bad, without condition.

ACT OF LOVE

Practice God's unconditional love for saints and sinners today. Remember that the Lord poured out the cup of his blood for ALL. See how many sinners you can collect into God's mercy today.

PRAYER OF FAITH

Father, you exist beyond anything I can think of you. You are amazing. You welcome the good and the bad. Welcome me. I'm not always as good as I ought to be, but I hope in your abiding love. Amen.

Saving Money, Killing Jesus

"But you are trying to kill me." JOHN 8:37

There's a lady at church who gives me money so I can give it to the poor. She figures, because of my work in the community, I'm much more likely to encounter people who really need help. Plus I think she's a little intimidated when it comes to dealing with needy people herself.

So I'm out in the parking lot of the supermarket with my shopping cart and this guy comes up to me and asks if I can help him out because he's trying to put together enough for a tank of gas. He points toward his vehicle, a dilapidated old pickup that looks like it needs a lot more than a tank of gas. And there was a woman and child in the front and furniture piled in the back. The guy was obviously moving. I gave him a dollar.

Later on it occurred to me that if the charity I showed him was any indication, it would take him two months to come up with enough for a tank of gas. And I had a pocketful of money from the lady at church!

Every time I embrace the world in some way with a choice of self over others, a choice of rejection over love, I kill Jesus in my heart. I put to death the one in me who is trying to save me, and others through me, by being for others what he is being for me. Yet in every moment Jesus accepts that I crucify him, reaches out in forgiveness, and offers me new life and the freedom that comes from knowing the truth about myself.

ACT OF LOVE

The truth will set you free, too. Today, at the end of the day, count how many times you may have crucified Jesus in your heart by being a child of the world. You'll be surprised.

PRAYER OF FAITH

O Lord Jesus, you gave yourself for me, yet I fail to give myself for others. Transform me by the power of your Spirit so that I might better serve you in this world. Amen.

The Lotto Prayer

"Amen, amen, I say to you, before Abraham came to be, I AM." JOHN 8:58

There was a guy who used to come to my church to pray every day. He approached me one day and asked, "Father, is it okay to ask God to give me the lottery number? I promised God I would give half my winnings to the church." I was inclined to join him in his prayer. But my answer was measured, for I was personally acquainted with the spirit of avarice in my own soul. "Tell you what," I said, "how about you give half of what you have now, and then maybe the Lord will give you the lottery number."

We both enjoyed a good laugh together. But I didn't see him around too much after that.

The encounter reminded me that the kingdom of God is a tough sell. When Jesus teaches the kingdom in parables, using finite images to explain infinite realities, I can sort of deal with it. But as soon as Jesus speaks directly of the eternal realities, i.e., "I AM," I run into difficulty. To say that God simply is makes my attachment to the things of this passing world seem rather ludicrous. Why on earth (literally) would I seek after wealth, authority, pleasure, comfort, and security, when all I would ever need, all I could ever want, is already given to me? What part of "the last shall be first" don't we understand?

ACT OF LOVE

Stop what you're doing right now and consider this: God is. Okay, you know that. But consider it. God is, right now, in you, knowing you, loving you, being with you. I pray that will blow your mind.

PRAYER OF FAITH

Eternal God, you are beyond what I can imagine. You live in infinite wonder, and your love for me is beyond my understanding. Can I spend a few moments with you today and consider your gracious love for me? Amen.

Not Jewish Enough

The Jews answered him, "We are not stoning you for a good work but
for blasphemy. You, a man, are making yourself God." JOHN 10:33

My friend Bob Schoen was finishing up his talk to my Catholic adult educa-
tion group. Bob is a devout Jew and author of the book, "What I Wish My
Christian Friends Knew about Judaism" (Loyola Press, 2004). After his talk
he invited questions. The first question was, "How come the Jews never accepted Jesus as the Messiah?"

Bob graciously and patiently explained how Jesus was just too far outside
the Jewish box for thoughtful Jews to accept him as the Messiah. The Christ,
for Jews, would have to be square in the middle of the box, unquestionably
orthodox, and not playing fast and loose with the law as Jesus did. Plus, he
would be a man and not God. The concept of man and God just never got
any traction in Jewish tradition.

It gives you an idea of how blessed we are to have two thousand years of
Catholic teaching behind our faith. Our faith in Jesus as God is taken for
granted. Imagine if we had to start from scratch like the Jewish disciples did.
I don't think it would have been so easy. As it is, we've never known God
to be anything other than Father, Son, and Holy Spirit. Perhaps the harder
thing to believe is that in Christ the divinity of God is wrapped up in our
own humanity. Jesus humbled himself to share in our humanity so that we
might have a share in his divinity.

ACT OF LOVE

Notice yourself today. Be aware of your life, your breathing, and your
heartbeat. From that perspective, be the eyes and ears and awareness
of God in the world today.

PRAYER OF FAITH

Father Creator, your Holy Spirit gives me life, and your Son, Jesus
Christ, rescues me from death. Thank you for your gracious gift. Amen.

One for All or All for One?

"It is better for you that one man should die instead of the people."   JOHN 11:50

I always ask children to pray for me because I know their prayers are heard by God. I ask old people and sick people to pray for me, too. And God knows I need their prayers if I am to be a good priest.

Caiaphas, the high priest of Jerusalem presiding over the deliberations concerning Jesus in the gospel story, unknowingly spoke a profound truth about the saving death of Jesus. But when your pastor is doing a poor job and things aren't going well, and you write to your bishop about the hurt and confusion your beloved parish is going through, and after repeated attempts to improve the situation fail, your bishop will sometimes react along the lines of what I call "the reverse Caiaphas principle." In other words, his decisions will be based on the notion that somehow it is better that many people should suffer for the sake of one man. That's when a parish is stuck with a pastor who tears down the faith of the people rather than builds it up. It happens.

Even though Jesus taught that the role of leadership in the community was service of the people, that role, in church as in politics, sometimes gets reversed. That's why we pray for our bishops and our clergy every day. Our priests need the prayer, love, and forgiveness of all and the new life offered by God in Christ.

ACT OF LOVE

Pray for your priests today. Pray for your bishop. Pray for the pope. Pray for all people in authority that they may serve the people they're responsible for and guide them with wisdom and gentleness.

PRAYER OF FAITH

O Lord, you sacrificed your only begotten Son so that all might live in the newness of life. Help our bishops and pastors to care for their flocks with tenderness. Amen.

Beatles Hymn Book

Jesus gave a loud cry and breathed his last.   MARK 15:37

"When I find myself in times of trouble, Mother Mary comes to me, speaking words of wisdom: 'Let it be.'"

Some may argue that this verse is from an unlikely source: Paul McCartney of the Beatles. Nevertheless, he draws the image from the gospels, namely Luke 1:38, "Let it be done unto me according to your word." It is a chilling passage, the total and complete surrender of Mary to the will of God. From that moment on, Mary committed herself to all that being called and chosen would mean: that the virgin would conceive, God would become human, the Word would be made flesh.

Once when I was doing the Stations of the Cross with a bunch of children, this little kid asked, "Why are they doing this to him?" "Oh," I said. "It was God's will that he suffer like this." The child thought for a moment, looking perplexed, then said, "I don't think I like God any more."

The child's response made me think: What actually do we mean by saying God willed that Jesus suffer and die? Maybe it's this: God so loved us that God became one of us to be with us, to join us in our humanity. God willingly endured all that being human meant, even suffering, even dying. He humbled himself to share in our humanity so that we might have a share in his divinity.

ACT OF LOVE

Got a problem today? When the spirit of trouble arises in your life, remember that God is with you, sharing your human weakness, suffering with you and for you.

PRAYER OF FAITH

Jesus Lord, you suffered and died for me. It is a mystery I find hard to comprehend. May this Holy Week be for me and my sisters and brothers a time of renewal and hope. Amen.

Salvation for a Quarter

"You always have the poor with you, but you do not always have me."
JOHN 12:8

A friend of mine lives in a large city and walks everywhere she goes. She likes to carry a pocketful of quarters because there are so many panhandlers who live and beg along the sidewalks where she travels. "A quarter isn't much," she says, "but they only ask for spare change."

A relatively inconspicuous line, but one of the most oft quoted of the gospels: "The poor you will always have with you." What makes this humble verse so frequently repeated? Regularly distorted, it serves as a handy rationale for ignoring the poor. "What's the point in helping the poor? Didn't Jesus say we'd always have the poor with us?" Right. But understood in the proper context, it simply means that there will be endless opportunities to help the poor. If I may borrow from another of the Lord's sayings, many are called to help the poor but few do.

There will always be those who lack the personal resources to manage their lives no matter how much money you give them, and there will always be those who are in need because others have failed to help. Who will I help today? Who will YOU help?

ACT OF LOVE

God will send the poor to you today so that you may have an opportunity to help. They will come to you as family, friend, or stranger. But you will have the means to help. Be ready today to do your part.

PRAYER OF FAITH

Heavenly Father, you give me time, abilities, and a certain measure of wealth. Help me today to use your gifts in the service of the poor. Amen.

FOJ (Friend of Judas)

"Amen, amen, I say to you, one of you will betray me." JOHN 13:21

Dennis is a good man who, like all of us, is also a sinner. "Why does God let me sin?" he laments. "Why, despite my best efforts, do I keep falling into sin?" It's a good question, one that is answered in the gospel readings of this Holy Week.

In the ironic twisting and turning of John's gospel, Jesus is pulled apart emotionally by the realization that he is going where his friends Peter and the others cannot follow. At the same time, his friend Judas is going where Jesus cannot follow: into the darkness of treachery and betrayal. It is curious that Jesus does not try to prevent Judas from doing what he is about to do. Instead he encourages him and hastens him along. Even in this dire strait, Jesus refuses to judge or condemn. Rather, he continues in friendship with Judas till the end. In Matthew's story, Jesus even exchanges a kiss with Judas and calls him, "friend" (Matthew 26:49–50).

Jesus is not naive; he is simply doing his job, revealing God's love at every turn, even the bad turns. Not even suffering and death will keep Jesus from his mission of showing God's love to all; even to Judas, even to my friend Dennis, even to me and to you.

ACT OF LOVE

If you are paying attention, you will discover yourself doing something sinful today. In your thoughts, in your words, in what you do, and in what you fail to do, you will encounter your own sinfulness. Let God know and allow God to forgive.

PRAYER OF FAITH

Father, what great love you show me. What an abundance of forgiveness you pour out in my life. Help me be grateful today for your mercy and compassion. Amen.

That'll Teach You

"The Son of Man indeed goes, as it is written of him, but woe to that man by whom the Son of Man is betrayed." MATTHEW 26:24

I remember once when I was very small, I was walking down the street with my mother. She was upset with me for some reason—I can't imagine why—and was walking very fast. My little legs couldn't keep up and eventually I tripped and fell, skinning my knee painfully. "That's God punishing you," my mother snapped, tugging me to my feet, "for not cleaning up your room like I told you." It was one of my earliest lessons in theology.

In a different way, we hear in today's gospel story Jesus predicting the punishment Judas will receive for his betrayal. But does that punishment come from God? Or is Judas making a bed that he will eventually have to lie in himself? Jesus welcomes Judas to the intimacy of table fellowship, even eating from the same dish as he. But Judas has chosen the path of treachery and betrayal, and this will lead to great pain for both his master and himself. God does not have to inflict any punishment on Judas; his actions have their own painful consequences.

If you put your hand in the fire it will get burned. Jesus accepts his own part in the suffering. He will pour out the cup of his blood for the sins of the world, including those of Judas. But the betrayer didn't bargain on the pain, only the silver.

ACT OF LOVE

Did you ever ask yourself, "Why is God punishing me?" Change your mind today. God doesn't do anything bad to us. We do bad things to ourselves and to each other.

PRAYER OF FAITH

You forgive all my sins, Almighty God, and keep me safe from evil.
Save me from the consequences of my own wrongdoing today, and may
I try with all my heart to correct my faults. Amen.

Dirty Feet

"If I, therefore, the master and teacher, have washed your feet,
you ought to wash one another's feet." JOHN 13:14

One sure sign of the coming of summer is that around this time of year I start wearing my sandals. And once I start wearing them, it is unlikely you'll see my shoes and socks again much before winter. But my feet sure get dirty. Exposed as I walk, they take on the dirt of a dirty world.

In John's gospel, the story of the first Eucharist is about washing dirty feet. Unlike the other gospels that include the bread and wine in their stories of the Last Supper, John includes no mention of what's on the menu. One reason for this startling absence may be that by the time this last gospel was written, the author assumed a common knowledge of the Eucharist as bread and wine.

No, John seems interested in presenting an understanding of what this meal means to the people who participate in it. Although all have bathed, all come to the supper with dirty feet. All have been washed clean in baptism, but all have weak human flesh and are therefore constantly tarnished by sin and in need of washing. When the community gathers to celebrate the Paschal mystery, the Lord is present, forgiving sins and imparting eternal life. As sinners are forgiven, so must sinners forgive others. "What I have done for you, you must do for each other." (Jn 13:15)

ACT OF LOVE

In the Creed we recite every Sunday, we say we believe in the forgiveness of sins. But we must live this faith every day. Who do you need to forgive today?

PRAYER OF FAITH

My Savior, you suffered and died on the cross for me so that my sins may be forgiven. Help me today to forgive those who trespass against me. Amen.

The Heavy Friend

*Carrying the cross himself, he went out to what is called the
Place of the Skull, in Hebrew, Golgotha.* JOHN 19:17

For Fran, being friends with Linda was a difficult proposition. Linda had issues. Her life was full of problems. When Fran was with Linda, she felt drained and put upon. But she stuck with Linda because they were friends. What else are friends for?

For Jesus as well as for us, the cross is the burden of being truly human. Jesus bound himself in love to his friends; coarse, difficult people, northerners with accents and crude ways. He sought out unruly people who were thickheaded and hard to handle: the inept fisherman, the radical insurgent, the traitor taxman, and the treacherous thief. But he bore them. He stuck with them. He wore them like flesh and he let them inside himself like blood. And it hurt. The heaviest, hardest burden he carried was his mortal humanity. In the end it is our own humanity that betrays us, judges us, condemns us, abandons us, and crucifies us.

But there is more. There is always more. The love of God is always with us, defending us, saving us, forgiving us, and raising us up. When all else fails, God continues. We came from God and we will return to God. God will not abandon us to death. On the last day, God will raise us up.

ACT OF LOVE

There is a cross you bear in your life that weighs heavily upon your shoulders. It may be a friend, a son or daughter, a parent, a spouse, or a coworker. Take up your cross today and follow in the footsteps of the One who bears the cross that is you.

PRAYER OF FAITH

Lord Jesus, you bore my sins so that I might be forgiven. You suffered and died for me so that I might live. Help me to bear the cross of my life today and follow you. Amen.

Blockbuster Liturgy

"Do not be amazed! You seek Jesus of Nazareth, the crucified.
He has been raised." MARK 16:6

A lady came up to me after the Easter Vigil once and gushed, "Oh Father, whenever I hear the story of Moses parting the Red Sea, I always think of Charlton Heston in *The Ten Commandments*." Four thousand years of salvation history, two thousand years of Christianity, weeks of preparation, and all she can think about is Charlton Heston? Okay. I'll accept that as a step in the right direction.

Our forty days of Lent conclude with the Easter Vigil. By the grace of God, our journey of forgiveness has been a fruitful one. Through fasting, prayer, and works of charity, we have, I hope, answered the Lord's call to repentance and received in return a newness of life. By dying with Christ, we hope to rise with him. It is in the Easter Vigil that we celebrate the fulfillment of all our hopes and dreams.

That is why this liturgy is so rich in story and symbol, word and sacrament: The fire, the light, the smoke, the song; the creation story, the Abraham story, the Exodus story, the visions of the prophets, the instruction of the apostle, the experience of the women at the tomb; water blessed, lives transformed, bread and wine offered, body and blood consumed—in all this a people are renewed and sent forth. Alleluia! Alleluia!

ACT OF LOVE

Bring a bell to the Easter Vigil. When the Gloria is sung and the bells are rung, ring your bell with the whole church as a sign of your joy that the glory of God is alive in you.

PRAYER OF FAITH

God, our Creator, so great is your love. May tonight's celebration ring throughout all the earth. By our lenten observance, may we rise with Christ to Easter joy. Amen.